A KID'S GUIDE TO
Understanding
the End Times

Tim LaHaye

Jerry B. Jenkins
with Chris Fabry

HARVEST HOUSE PUBLISHERS

EUGENE, OREGON

Cover by Terry Dugan Design, Minneapolis, Minnesota

If you'd like to know more about Tim LaHaye or Jerry B. Jenkins, please visit their websites: timlahaye.com and jerryjenkins.com.

A KID'S GUIDE TO UNDERSTANDING THE END TIMES
Copyright © 2004 by Tim LaHaye, Jerry B. Jenkins, and Chris Fabry
Published by Harvest House Publishers
Eugene, Oregon 97402
www.harvesthousepublishers.com

This text has been adapted from *Understanding Bible Prophecy for Yourself* by Tim LaHaye (Harvest House Publishers, 1998, 2001).

Library of Congress Cataloging-in-Publication Data

LaHaye, Tim F.
    A kid's guide to understanding the end times/Tim LaHaye and Jerry B. Jenkins with Chris Fabry.
       p. cm.
    ISBN 0-7369-1245-2 (pbk.)
  1. Bible—Prophecies—End of the world—Juvenile literature. 2. End of the world—Biblical teaching—Juvenile literature.   I. Jenkins, Jerry B.   II. Fabry, Chris, 1961-. III. Title.
    BS649.E63L343 2004
    236—dc22   2004000757

Printed in the United States of America

04 05 06 07 08 09 10 11 /BP-KB/ 10 9 8 7 6 5 4 3 2 1

Contents

Urgent!

☆　☆　☆

Judd ran upstairs and checked Marcie's room first. She was the persnickety one, the one who always kept her room just so, dolls lined up in a row, her schoolbooks and the next day's clothes laid out neatly. Two tiny barrettes lay in the dent in the pillow her dark-haired head had left. Judd pulled back the covers, revealing her nightie.

In Marc's room, which was almost as messy as Judd's own, he found socks and underpants in the bed.

…He slipped into his parents' bedroom, where the curtains were closed and it was dark…Judd was stunned to see that his parents' bed was still made. Could it be? Was it possible they had not been taken?

He ran to the living room, where the truth quickly became clear. The phone receiver was on the floor. From the positions of his parents' sets of clothes, it was obvious they had changed back into them when they realized they might have to drive somewhere to look for him. His dad's jeans and pullover shirt and shoes were in a pile near the phone…His mother had told him and told him that Jesus was coming again and that it could happen in Judd's *lifetime. He knew that was what his church taught, but it had seemed so preposterous. Well, not any more. It had happened, and he had been left behind.*

The Vanishings
(Left Behind: The Kids #1)

☾ ☾ ☾ ☾ ☾

Millions of young people have read the Left Behind: The Kids® series that Jerry B. Jenkins and Chris Fabry wrote for me (Tim). Perhaps you were one of them. It would seem that young people hunger to know about the future. And since you're reading this book, you want to know more about the future too.

God created each of us with a soul—the part of us that is going to live forever and longs to know what's ahead. The good news is that God has given answers about the future in His Word. We call them "prophecies." A "prophecy" is when God tells us what will happen in the future. At the time they were written, more than 1,000 passages in the Bible were prophecies. More than half of the Bible prophecies have *already* come true, and the rest will come true in the future!

I'm convinced there has never been a more urgent time for God's followers to know His wonderful plan for the future. Jesus warned His disciples that there would be liars, false teachers, and false prophets in the last days. That's why we need to study God's Word carefully. If we are living in the last days, we need to know what to expect so we're not fooled or tricked when these liars and false prophets say *they* know about the future.

Good to Know

A "prophecy" is a Scripture verse or passage where God tells us what will happen in the future.

That's what this book is all about—to help you know God's plan for the future. It's an exciting subject, and I pray it will help you live every day for Jesus.

In this book, you won't just *read* about Bible prophecy, you'll *study* it for yourself as well. You'll discover the basics, find answers, and be able to help other people understand what God's Word really teaches about the future.

The Bible challenges us to correctly explain the Word of truth (2 Timothy 2:15). This book will help you correctly explain the truths of prophecy! I hope you're excited about what's ahead.

1

Let's Go!

☆ ☆ ☆

"People are missing," she said. "Disappeared. Vanished. Right out of their clothes. Watch the news. It's all over the world. Three trailers here burned to the ground. Lots of people lost family. Mrs. Johnson vanished late last night drivin' her husband home from the bus stop. He couldn't grab the wheel in time, and the car hit a tree. He's hurt real bad."

"Shelly, are you high? Drunk? Walking in your sleep? What?"

The Vanishings
(Left Behind: The Kids #1)

☾ ☾ ☾ ☾ ☾

Though some people think prophecy is difficult to understand and avoid it, I believe this is the perfect time to study "future things." If false teachers are coming, or are already here, Christians need to know *more* about prophecy, not less, so they can be armed with the truth and protect themselves from false teachers.

Think of this: One of the greatest teachers in church history, the apostle Paul (remember him? He met Jesus on the road to Damascus), thought prophecy was important to teach young Christians. Look at what he says:

> Now, brothers, about times and dates we do not need to write to you, for you know very well that the day of the Lord will come like a thief in the night. While people are saying, "Peace and safety," destruction will come on them suddenly, as labor pains on a pregnant woman, and they will not escape.
>
> But you, brothers, are not in darkness so that this day should surprise you like a thief. You are all sons of the light and sons of the day. We do not belong to the night or to the darkness (1 Thessalonians 5:1-5).

Paul clearly believed young Christians could handle such topics as "the day of the Lord," which is a reference to the second coming of Jesus. Later in 1 Thessalonians, Paul gives the most detailed description of the coming of Christ for His church in the whole Bible! Then in 2 Thessalonians, written a short time later, Paul taught about the coming of the Antichrist and other future events. Paul didn't ignore prophecy. Instead, he taught it so it would challenge believers to live for Jesus every day.

It's true that some details of prophecy are hard to understand, but the basics aren't. By the time you finish this book, you'll know more about...

☆ the return of Jesus

☆ the Tribulation

☆ the Millennial kingdom (or the 1,000-year reign of Jesus)

☆ the glorious appearing of Christ to rule over the earth

☆ and eternity!

Knowing God's plan for the future will help you live the kind of life that will cause God to say to you on judgment day, "Well done, good and faithful servant" (Matthew 25:23).

A Big Difference

While many books on prophecy only try to get you to believe what the author believes, I want *you* to explore New and Old Testament prophecies and figure out what *God* is saying about the future. You'll answer questions and let God speak to you. I'll also give you my understanding and sometimes share other explanations by Bible-believing Christians.

Remember, the Bible was written to ordinary people like you and me. You can understand what God is saying, including the prophecy passages, because you have the help of the Holy Spirit. Jesus promised, "When he, the Spirit of truth, comes, he will guide you into all truth...and he will tell you what is yet to come" (John 16:13).

You've got your work cut out for you, but I know you can do it! And we're going to start with *why Christians should study prophecy.*

2

Why Do You Need to Know About Prophecy?

☆ ☆ ☆

Dr. Rosenzweig talked of his former student Tsion Ben-Judah. Vicki's heart sank when Chaim referred to Tsion's belief in Jesus as "madness." When the host tried to interrupt him, Dr. Rosenzweig said, "I have earned the right to another minute or so.

"Ben-Judah was ridiculed for his belief that scriptural prophecy would actually happen. He said an earthquake would come. It came. He said hail and rain and fire would scorch the plants. They did. He said things would fall from the sky, poisoning water, killing people, sinking ships. They fell.

"He said the sun and the moon and the stars would be stricken and that the world would be one-third darker. Well, I am finished. I don't know what to make of it except that I feel a bigger fool every day. And let me just add, I want to know what Dr. Tsion Ben-Judah says is coming next! Don't you?"

Darkening Skies
(Left Behind: The Kids #18)

☾ ☾ ☾ ☾ ☾

God has given us three important signs that He is a supernatural God:

★ creation

★ Jesus Christ

★ the Bible

Creation shows us God exists (Romans 1:19, 20). Because it's impossible to get order from disorder, something from nothing, it's clear that the well-designed universe we live in had a designer. And that designer was God.

Jesus Christ, the most famous and important man who ever lived, is the evidence of both God's existence and His incredible love for people. For God not only sent His Son into the world to identify with mankind, but to *die* for mankind, so that men and women, boys and girls, could have their sins forgiven and then enjoy God forever.

But the best way for us to know and understand God today is the **Bible**. Creation can't tell us everything about God; it doesn't show His forgiveness, for example. Jesus showed us by His words and actions who God is, and His teachings were the exact expression of God. Yet we come to know Jesus through the written Word of God, through the Bible. We would know very little about Christ without the Bible.

Good to Know

The Bible is filled with prophecies that have already come true.

One way we know the Bible is true is by looking at prophecies that have come true. People can try, but only God can tell us the future. The Bible is filled with prophecies that have already come true. The fact of fulfilled prophecy is how we can know Jesus Christ is the Messiah: More than 100 prophecies of His first coming to earth were fulfilled in His birth, life, and death!

That's how we can be sure He's coming again. There are eight times as many prophecies about Christ's *second* coming as for His *first* coming! That truth is exciting—but it doesn't help unless you study it.

There are other reasons for studying this very important subject. Think about these:

1. Prophecy must be important because God put so much of it in the Bible.

The Bible is not just one book but a library of books, and many of those books contain prophecy. Of God's 66 books of the Bible to us, most were written by prophets. There are 16 books of prophecy in the Old Testament. In the New Testament, God used all but four books to talk about prophecy. Because so much of the Bible includes prophecy, it's clear God wants His children to study it.

2. Prophecy shows us Jesus as He really is.

I've always loved prophecy because it shows Jesus for who He really is. In the Gospels we see His humility, His lowly birth, suffering, and death. But the second coming is different! Never again will Jesus Christ suffer at the hands of men or be ruled by them. The next time He comes it will be "in power and great glory" as "King of kings and Lord of lords." At that coming the Bible says that "every eye will see him" (Revelation 1:7) and that "every knee [will] bow, in heaven and on earth and under the earth, and every tongue [will] confess that Jesus Christ is Lord, to the glory of God the Father" (Philippians 2:10-11).

3. Understanding prophecy helps you know truths from lies.

Scripture says that in the last days more and more people will teach things from the Bible that aren't true. The best defense against this is to "put on the full armor of God so that you can take your stand against the devil's schemes" (Ephesians 6:11). Jesus predicted that these false christs and false prophets will be able to perform great signs and miracles to try to trick true believers.

There once was a man who sold 300,000 books claiming Jesus was coming back in September of 1988. The date came and went, and the man decided he had missed the date by exactly one year—so he put out another book. Of course, he was wrong! A good rule to follow about any teacher of prophecy who sets a date for the coming of Christ is this: *Don't believe him!* Jesus said in Matthew 24:36: "No one knows about that day or hour, not even the angels in heaven, nor the Son, but only the Father." The best way to avoid being tricked by the false teachers is to understand prophecy.

4. Prophecy offers hope in a hopeless time.

People can't live without hope, and this world has very little to offer. We see wars and hatred between people. The world wants peace but can't find it. But people who study prophecy aren't afraid because they know what our loving God has planned for the future. They believe with all their heart that Jesus is coming again. Early Christians had a greeting we could use today. They would say, "Maranatha" (1 Corinthians 16:22), which means "O Lord, come." Students of prophecy don't dread what's ahead because we know the One who holds the future.

The sad truth is that the worst days in world history are yet to come. Jesus warned that there would be a time of "great tribulation, such as has not been since the beginning of the world until this time, no, nor ever shall be" (Matthew 24:21 NKJV). But if you understand prophecy, you don't have to worry. You have a place in God's plan. And that hope in God comes when you study His Word and understand everything He promised will come true.

If we begin to see the world merge into one government and one leader arises, Christians don't need to be anxious. This is just another sign that the coming of the Lord is near. Christians can know a "peace that passes all understanding" as a result of knowing the prophecies of the Bible.

Bible prophecy tells us that Jesus will destroy Satan. In Revelation 20:3 we learn Jesus will chain him in the bottomless pit, where he will "deceive the nations no more." Christians who know prophecy can face what seems to be a scary future with peaceful confidence. No matter how bad it gets, we know Jesus will take care of everything.

3

Jesus Is Coming Again—You Can Be Sure of It!

☆　☆　☆

Someone brought a bottle of water and Micah showed Nicolae it had turned to blood. Nicolae said, "I want my people healthy and my water pure."

"You know the price."

"Specifics."

"Israeli Jews who have chosen to believe Jesus the Christ is their Messiah must be allowed to leave before you punish anyone for not taking your mark. And devout Orthodox Jews must be allowed a place where they can worship after you have defiled their temple."

Judd's mind reeled. He was watching prophecy being fulfilled before his very eyes.

Murder in the Holy Place
(Left Behind: The Kids #30)

☾　☾　☾　☾　☾

Let's get to work learning more about the second coming of Christ. Did you know it is talked about eight times more in the entire Bible than His first coming? It's true! In fact, the only truth mentioned more in the New Testament is the teaching on salvation! Jesus' coming is mentioned 318 times in the New Testament alone, and all the authors of the New Testament talk about it.

To help you study this truth for yourself, grab a Bible and look up the following verses. Then, with a pencil or pen, fill in the study guide. Don't try to look for hidden meanings in the verses—just answer the questions and write your answers down. Here we go.

The Certainty of Christ's Second Coming

Matthew 24. Describe what Christ's second coming will be like in—

verse 27:_____

verse 30:_____

Mark 13:27. What will Christ do when He comes?

_____

John 14:1-3. What specific promise did Jesus make here?

_____

_____

Acts 1:10-11. What does the angel promise?

_____

Philippians 3:20-21. Where will Christ come from, and what will He do when He comes?

_____

_____

2 Thessalonians 2:1. What is the subject of this chapter?

_____

James 5:8. How should we live as we await Christ's return?

_____

Jude 14-15. List three things this passage states about Jesus' return.

1. _____

2. _____

3. _____

A Guided Tour

These are only a few of the 318 New Testament references about Christ's second coming. For more, here's a quick tour of the New Testament.

Matthew. Two entire chapters, 24 and 25, are devoted to the second coming of Jesus. Often called the "Olivet Discourse," this message was delivered just before Jesus' death. Other than Revelation, this sermon gives the most important and complete timeline of future events found in the Bible.

Mark. Mark devotes chapter 13 to the Olivet Discourse, ending with the second coming of Christ.

Luke. This great first-century historian and doctor included the second coming prophecies in chapters 17 and 21 of this book. He wrote, "They will see the Son of Man [Jesus] coming in a cloud with power and great glory" (21:27).

John. The "beloved disciple," who outlived all the other apostles, wrote his book about 50 years after Christ went back into heaven. He gives one of the clearest promises to come from Jesus' lips on this subject:

> Do not let your hearts be troubled. Trust in God; trust also in me. In my Father's house are many rooms; if it were not so, I would have told you. I am going there

to prepare a place for you. And if I go and prepare a place for you, *I will come back* and take you to be with me that you also may be where I am (14:1-3, emphasis added).

Acts. Luke also wrote about the Holy Spirit's work through the apostles, and this book contains several promises of Christ's second coming. Two angels announce to Jesus' disciples: "Men of Galilee...why do you stand here looking into the sky? This same Jesus, who has been taken from you into heaven, will come back in the same way you have seen him go into heaven" (1:11).

Good to Know

The Bible uses many different words and phrases to talk about Jesus coming again. Look for words and phrases like these...

"come back"	*"when he appears"*
"the day of the Lord"	*"the Lord's coming"*
"his coming"	*"the appearing"*
"his appearing"	*"the glorious appearing"*

Thirteen Letters of Paul. The writings of the apostle Paul had a huge impact on the early believers. Paul taught deep truths, gave practical instruction, corrected people, and showed how to live the Christian life. He talked about important things like baptism 13 times and communion twice, but he mentioned the second coming of Jesus 50 times! That's a lot! (If you want to know more about what Paul had to say on Jesus coming again, see "Digging Deeper" on page 26 at the end of this chapter.)

Hebrews. One of the promises of Jesus' return found in this book states: "So Christ sacrificed once to take away the sins of many people; and he will appear a second time, not to bear sin, but to bring salvation to those who are waiting for him" (9:28).

James. This little book, which challenges Christians to show their faith by their works, ends with a strong plea: "Be patient and stand firm, because the Lord's coming is near" (5:8).

Peter. Writing to people who were being persecuted, the apostle Peter challenged the elders to be faithful leaders on the basis of the Lord's coming: "And when the Chief Shepherd appears, you will receive the crown of glory that will never fade away" (1 Peter 5:4). Peter's second letter contains a long prophecy about the rise of people who will make fun of Christianity just before Christ's coming. He promises that "the day of the Lord will come like a thief" (2 Peter 3:10).

First John. This beautiful letter brings assurance of salvation and confidence to us, but it also challenges us to live right because Christ could return at any time. One example is this: "Now, dear children, continue in him, so that when he appears we may be confident and unashamed before him at his coming" (2:28).

Jude. This tiny, one-chapter book contains a quotation from Enoch, a man who knew God well and lived before Noah's flood, then suddenly went directly to be with God. Genesis 5:24 says, "Enoch walked with God; then he was no more, because God took him away." Some prophecy teachers think Enoch's experience is a lot like what will happen to Christians just before the Tribulation, when Jesus will suddenly take Christians off this earth to be with Himself (see 1 Thessalonians 4:13-18 and 1 Corinthians 15:51-52). Before Enoch suddenly went to God, he gave this inspired prophecy: "Enoch, the seventh from Adam, prophesied about these men: 'See, the Lord is coming with thousands upon thousands of his holy ones to judge everyone, and to convict all the ungodly of all the ungodly acts they have done in the ungodly way, and of all the harsh words ungodly sinners have spoken against him'" (Jude 14-15).

Revelation. The Bible ends with an entire book filled with prophecies about the second coming. These prophecies talk about events predicted in the first century and all the way until the end of the world.

These are just a few references to the Lord's second coming, but there are many more. If you believe the Bible, you must believe Jesus is coming again.

Digging Deeper

As I mentioned earlier in this chapter, the apostle Paul talked a lot about Jesus coming again. If you want to dig deeper, check out these verses and see for yourself what Paul had to say!

Paul wrote to young believers in 1 Thessalonians and referred to the second coming of Christ in every chapter (see 1:10; 2:19; 3:13; 4:13-18; 5:2,23)! He went into greater detail in 2 Thessalonians (see 1:7-10; 2:1-12; 3:5).

All but two of Paul's letters contain one or more references to the second coming. In Romans 11:26 and in 14:10 Paul talks about the judgment seat of Christ. That judgment is described in detail in 1 Corinthians 3:9-15. Then in 1 Corinthians 15 Paul describes the resurrection of the body and gives details of the rapture in verses 50-58 (we're going to talk about what the rapture is in the next chapter). He also refers to some of these same second coming truths in 2 Corinthians 1:14 and 5:10. Ephesians presents the Christian "in the heavenly realms" (1:3), and "the day of redemption" (4:30) can only mean the day of deliverance through Christ's return. Philippians contains several references to the Lord's coming, the best of which is Philippians 3:20-21:

> But our citizenship is in heaven. And we eagerly await a Savior from there, the Lord Jesus Christ, who, by the power that enables him to bring everything under his control, will transform our lowly bodies so that they will be like his glorious body.

A thrilling promise appears in Colossians: "When Christ, who is your life, appears, then you will also appear with him in glory" (3:4).

Like 1 and 2 Thessalonians, the letters to Timothy provide many references to the second coming of Christ. And 2 Timothy 1:10 and 4:1,8 refer to "the appearing" and "his appearing."

The book of Titus contains the advice of an older, wise servant of God to a young preacher on how to conduct the work of the Lord in the church. Paul challenges Titus to teach people "to live self-controlled, upright and godly lives in this present age, while we wait for the blessed hope—the glorious appearing of our great God and Savior, Jesus Christ" (2:12-13).

When all the books of Paul are considered, we find that only two of 13 don't mention the second coming, and they are Galatians and Philemon. There is no question the apostle Paul was absolutely certain that his Lord and Savior was coming back to this earth again.

4

What's the "Second Coming"?

☆ ☆ ☆

Lionel kept feeding Sam information and scripture. Like other new believers he had known, Sam was like a sponge. He couldn't get enough teaching about Jesus and the Bible.

Attack of Apollyon
(Left Behind: The Kids # 19)

There are two concepts you need to know when you talk about Jesus' "second coming":

☆ the rapture

☆ His glorious appearing

These events make up the two parts to the second coming. First, the rapture. Jesus will come suddenly in the air to take believers to His Father's house. Second, His glorious appearing. Jesus will finish His second coming by returning to earth gloriously and publicly in great power to set up His kingdom. We're going to take a closer look at these two events and see how together they are called the second coming.

Now You See Us, Now You Don't

The first part of Jesus' second coming is "in the air" for believers; it will be a great blessing to all who participate in it. We call this "the rapture," based on the Greek word *harpazo* in 1 Thessalonians 4:17, which means "to be caught up." The same word is used in Acts 8:39 and describes how the Holy Spirit "took Philip away" after he baptized the Ethiopian. "Rapture" has come to refer to the part of Jesus' return when He appears in the air just for Christians.

Are you wondering about Christians who have died before the rapture takes place? The Bible tells us they will be resurrected (brought back from the dead) right before the rapture. The rapture will be a time of reuniting both dead believers and those who are alive and here on earth. They all will "meet the Lord in the air" (1 Thessalonians 4:17) and then be with Jesus forever. It's going to be incredible!

Let's take a look at the Bible verses that talk about the rapture.

The Rapture According to 1 Thessalonians 4:13-18

Grab your Bible and find 1 Thessalonians 4:13-18. It's one of the best descriptions of the rapture we have in the Bible. Answer these questions and you'll know even more!

Verse 13. List Paul's two purposes for telling us about the rapture.

1. We do not want you to be _____ about those who fall asleep. (The phrase "those who fall asleep" here means Christians who have died.)

2. We do not want you to _____ like the rest of men, who have no hope.

Verse 14. Whom did Paul say Jesus would bring when He comes again?

_____

Verse 15. Where did Paul get this teaching?

According to _____

What is the event Paul is describing?

the _____ of the _____

Verse 16. List the three things that happen when the Lord comes down from heaven.

1. _____

2. _____

3. _____

Who responds first?

_____

Verse 17. List three things that happen in sequence.

1. Those who are still alive will be _____ up in the _____.

2. Meet the _____ in the

   _____.

3. Be with the _____ forever.

Verse 18. Why did Paul tell us about the rapture?

_____

The Rapture According to 1 Corinthians 15:50-58

These Bible verses provide more details about what will happen during the rapture.

Verse 51. List two parts of a "mystery" that Paul reveals.

1. We will not all _____ .

2. We will all be _____ .
    (Remember, "sleep" here means "die.")

Verse 52. How fast will this change occur?

_____

What will happen when the trumpet sounds?

_____

Verse 58. What does Paul encourage us to do, knowing that someday death will be swallowed up in victory and we will all be changed?

1. Stand _____ .

2. Let nothing move _____ .

3. Always give yourselves fully to the
    _____ of the _____ .

Jesus Talks About the Rapture

Jesus talked about the rapture only once. All His other teachings on His return have to do with the second part (His glorious appearing)—the literal, physical return when

He will set up His kingdom. However, the day before Jesus died on the cross, He prepared His disciples to function during His absence and comforted them with these words:

> Do not let your hearts be troubled. Trust in God; trust also in me. In my Father's house are many rooms; if it were not so, I would have told you. I am going there to prepare a place for you. And if I go and prepare a place for you, I will come back and take you to be with me that you also may be where I am (John 14:1-3).

Underline the part of John 14:1-3 that talks about Jesus coming back for us. That's the rapture!

Part 2: When *Everyone* Will See Jesus

The second part of the Lord's second coming is the public appearance of Christ to earth. At that time He will set up His earthly kingdom. We call this "the glorious appearing of Christ." At that time "every eye will see him" (Revelation 1:7), and those who rejected Him will be very, very sad because they will finally realize who He really is and that it is now too late to accept Him by faith as Lord and Savior.

This second part of Jesus' coming is the one mentioned most in the Old and New Testaments. It is the event that all the prophets of Israel looked forward to and is the one the disciples had in mind when they asked Jesus, "What will be *the* sign of your coming and of the end of the age?" (Matthew 24:3).

We're going to look at Jesus' glorious appearing in more depth in chapter 7, but for now, let's go through a couple of the Bible passages that teach about this event, just to help us understand what it means.

The Glorious Appearing According to Matthew 24:29-31

Take a few minutes and read what Jesus had to say in Matthew 24:29-31, then answer these questions.

Verse 30. What will all the nations of the earth do when the Son of Man (another name for Jesus) appears in the sky?

_____

What will they see the Son of Man coming on?

_____

And how will He be coming?

With _____ and great _____

The Glorious Appearing According to Revelation 19:11-16

The apostle John gives probably one of the most graphic descriptions in the whole Bible of Jesus' glorious appearing.

Read his incredible words for yourself, and then answer these questions.

Verse 11. John saw a rider on a white horse. This rider is none other than Jesus Himself. What two names did John give Him?

_____ and _____

Verse 16. There is another name for Jesus written on His robe and on His thigh. What is it?

_____

Two Parts Equal One Whole

Now we can see that there are two parts to Jesus' second coming. The first part, the rapture, is when Jesus takes up Christians to be with Him, and the second part, the glorious appearing, is when Jesus comes to the world to judge unbelievers.

The chart on page 37 shows how these events fit together. After the rapture, the Lord remains "in the air," where He judges Christians and they receive their rewards (that's our next chapter!). Then, after this time of judgment (we're not told how long this is), Jesus finishes His second coming by coming to the earth "in power and great glory, with the holy angels" to rule and reign during what Scripture calls the "kingdom age."

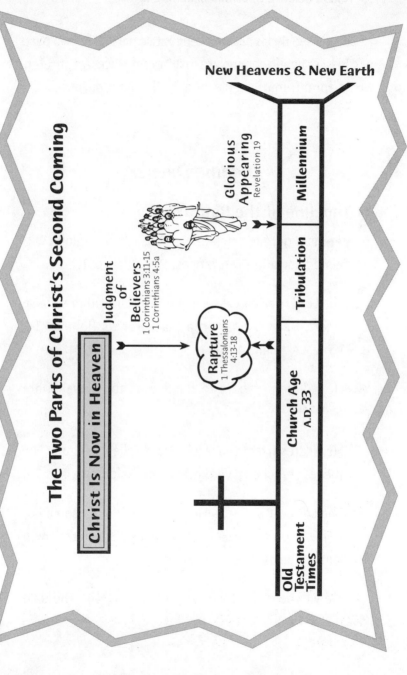

The Two Parts of Christ's Second Coming

Christ Is Now in Heaven

Judgment of Believers
1 Corinthians 3:11-15
1 Corinthians 4:5a

Rapture
1 Thessalonians
4:13-18

Glorious Appearing
Revelation 19

New Heavens & New Earth

Old Testament Times

Church Age
A.D. 33

Tribulation

Millennium

So you see this is all one event in two parts. The two parts of Christ's second coming are in different places, at different times, for different people, and for different purposes.

Digging Deeper

A Timeline of the Rapture

Here is a detailed timeline of the rapture, along with the related Scripture references. Check 'em out!

1. The Lord Himself will descend from His Father's house, where He is preparing a place for us (John 14:1-3; 1 Thessalonians 4:16).

2. He will come again to receive us to Himself (John 14:1-3).

3. He will resurrect those who have fallen asleep in Him (believers who have died—1 Thessalonians 4:14,15).

4. The Lord will shout as He descends ("loud command," 1 Thessalonians 4:16). All this takes place in the "twinkling of an eye" (1 Corinthians 15:52).

5. We will hear the voice of the archangel (1 Thessalonians 4:16).

6. We will also hear the trumpet call of God (1 Thessalonians 4:16).

7. The dead in Christ will rise first (1 Thessalonians 4:16,17).

8. Then we who are alive and remain will be changed (1 Corinthians 15:51,53).

9. We will be caught up (raptured) together (1 Thessalonians 4:17).

10. We will be caught up in the clouds (where dead and living believers will have a tremendous reunion— 1 Thessalonians 4:17).

11. We will meet Jesus in the air (1 Thessalonians 4:17).

12. Christ will receive us to Himself and take us to the Father's house (John 14:3).

13. "And so we will be with the Lord forever" (1 Thessalonians 4:17).

14. After Christ calls believers to Himself, they will stand before the judgment seat of Christ (Romans 14:10; 2 Corinthians 5:10), described in detail in 1 Corinthians 3:11-15. This judgment prepares Christians for...

15. The marriage of the Lamb. Before Christ returns to earth in power and great glory, He will meet His bride, the church, and the marriage supper will take place. In the meantime, after the church is raptured, the world will suffer God's anger, which our Lord called "the great tribulation" (Matthew 24:21 NKJV).

5

Seeing Jesus for the First Time

☆ ☆ ☆

"Remember Judd, she's not dead. If everything we believe is true, and we both know it is, she's in heaven."

"I know," he said, sitting on the couch and sighing. "But she might as well be dead. She's dead to me. I won't see her again."

"Not here, anyway," Vicki agreed, "but in heaven or when Jesus comes back."

Second Chance
(Left Behind: The Kids #2)

☾ ☾ ☾ ☾ ☾

Most Christians look forward to that incredible day when they will see Jesus. As we have already seen, God's plan for us is to meet our dead loved ones and friends "in the clouds" first, then to meet the Lord "in the air." That's the rapture.

Like many Christians, I have two parents I long to meet in the clouds, along with many friends. But meeting the Lord who died for us, forgave us, and saved us will be an even greater moment.

However, right after that event we will be judged by Him! Every Christian will stand before Jesus. Few Christians ever think about that. When Jesus comes in the rapture, He is going to judge His followers by examining their works and motives.

Remember, this judgment won't be about whether or not the person is saved because only saved people will be involved in the rapture. It's also not a judgment for sins committed before we became believers because Jesus took care of those on the cross. Instead, this judgment is to determine the rewards that we will receive for our faithful service after we were saved. Let's take a look at what this judgment is and what the rewards are.

The Judgment of Reward—1 Corinthians 3:9-15

The most detailed description of this coming judgment appears in 1 Corinthians 3:9-15. Look at the timeline on page 44. You'll see that this "Judgment of Reward" happens after the rapture.

What three things does Paul call Christians (verse 9)?

1. _____

2. _____

3. _____

List the six symbols Paul uses for good works in verse 12 (I've given you the first one).

1. _____ *gold* _____

2. _____

3. _____

4. _____

5. _____

6. _____

What will test those works (verse 13)?

It will be revealed with _____ , and the _____ will test the quality of each man's work.

What happens if a believer's works survive the test (verse 14)?

_____

What happens if they don't (verse 15)?

_____

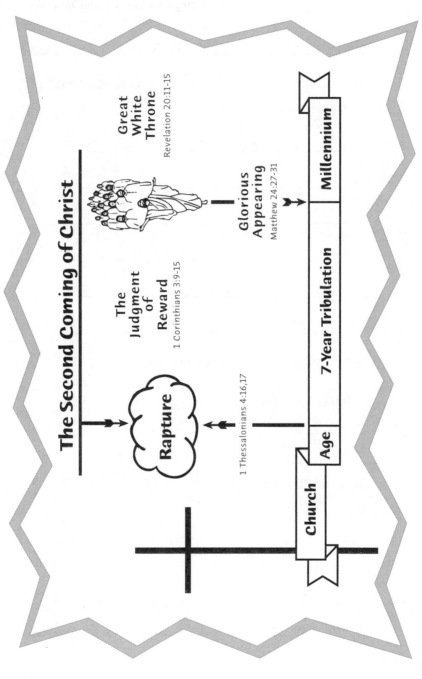

Understanding What "Good Works" Means

Here's a very important concept for you to know: Good works do *not* save us. Only believing in Jesus does that. We are saved "by grace...through faith—and this not from yourselves, it is the gift of God—not by works, so that no one can boast" (Ephesians 2:8-9).

Many Christians, however, then think they don't really have to serve God. They accept His salvation as a gift and do nothing to serve Him. Unfortunately, they do not pay attention to the very next verse: "We are God's workmanship, created in Christ Jesus to do good works, which God prepared in advance for us to do" (Ephesians 2:10).

We are "created in Christ Jesus to do good works." It is obvious that Jesus expects His children to work for Him after they have been given salvation. In fact, our rewards in the next life depend on the way we serve Him in this one.

At the "Judgment of Reward," Jesus will take a look at all we've done for Him and test our works with His holy "fire." The works that won't survive this fire are those that were not done with the right spirit or motive. To everyone else, it might look like we're doing great things for Jesus, but God's test will reveal what sort of works we have done, whether good or bad. Were we doing our works from a pure heart?

Ultimately, how all this will turn out is known only to God. What's important is the fact that God's work should be done in God's way—with a pure heart and a desire to honor Him.

The Bible says our faithful service will be rewarded with crowns. A crown is a symbol of rulership and these crowns are given on the basis of faithful service. The apostle Paul challenged Timothy, "Discharge all the duties of your ministry" (2 Timothy 4:5). In other words, we are to take advantage of all opportunities to use our talents to serve God while we are on earth. Any faithful Christian can earn at least one of these crowns, and many will earn several.

What About You?

The judgment seat of Christ will be an exciting experience for the faithful child of God—which I hope you are. The purpose of this judgment is to reward faithful servants with job assignments for the Millennial kingdom. You will serve Christ during that period in direct proportion to the way you have served Him in this life. It is entirely up to you how you will spend those 1,000 years!

Our Lord will be the last world emperor and His rule will extend into eternity. However, as we shall see, His kingdom will be unique. It will feature peace and prosperity, the curse on the earth will be lifted, and man's cruelty will end. For the first time since the Garden of Eden, man will love his neighbor as himself.

It's going to be a wonderful, beautiful time. By serving God faithfully now, you'll be ready to serve Him faithfully in the future.

Digging Deeper

The Scripture mentions five different crowns available to believers.

The Crown of Righteousness—2 Timothy 4:8

The Crown that Lasts Forever—1 Corinthians 9:25-27

The Crown of Life—James 1:12; Revelation 2:10

The Crown of Rejoicing—1 Thessalonians 2:19

The Crown of Glory—1 Peter 5:4

6

The Really Tough
Times Ahead

Vicki looked up, her face white with fear. She knew some words in Bible prophecy stood for other things, but these words seemed clear.

"I'm not a Bible teacher or a scholar," Rayford said, "but I ask you, is there anything difficult to understand about a passage that begins, 'Behold, there was a great earthquake'? Bruce has carefully charted these events. I believe the Four Horsemen of the Apocalypse are at full gallop. And I also think the fifth seal, the tribulation martyrs whose souls are under the altar, has begun."

It all fits, Vicki thought.

Into the Storm
(Left Behind: The Kids #11)

here are tough times coming to planet earth. The Bible calls this the "Tribulation." If you have read any of the Left Behind: The Kids books, you know how scary the

Tribulation period will be—earthquakes, terrifying horse-men, demon locusts, and more. The Old Testament prophets, particularly Daniel, had much to say about that time period, and the book of Revelation uses 13 chapters to describe it in detail. Jesus said of this time, "There will be great distress, unequaled from the beginning of the world until now" (Matthew 24:21).

What's important is that in the Bible, there is more space given to the Tribulation than any subject except sal-vation and the promise of Christ's second coming. It is mentioned at least 49 times in the Old Testament and at least 15 times in the New Testament.

What the Bible describes happening during the Tribu-lation has never happened, so it must still be in the future. The Tribulation is commonly considered to be seven years long based on Daniel's vision described in Daniel 9:24-27 (yes, that would be the same Daniel who spent the night in the lion's den).

Who's Going to Be Here?

Many Christians believe the rapture is going to happen before the Tribulation, and they say believers won't be going through the Tribulation. Other Christians believe the rapture will happen halfway through the Tribulation and say believers will go through the first half of the Tribula-tion. And still other Christians believe that the rapture won't happen until the end of the Tribulation, meaning believers will experience all of the Tribulation. While the Scripture is very clear on the fact that Christ will come again, it is not as clear whether He will come before, during, or after the Tribulation for those who believe in Him.

I personally believe the rapture will happen *before* the Tribulation begins. I've studied the passages about the end times a lot, and this view fits what all the Scriptures have to say about this topic better than the other two views. And it is a commonsense view that brings comfort to the hearts of believers, which is one of the main purposes for teaching end-times prophecy (1 Thessalonians 4:18).

From everything I've studied, I've concluded that if you're a believer in Jesus Christ when the rapture occurs, you will *not* be here for the Tribulation.

Why Would God Cause Such Terrible Times?

You might be wondering why God will allow the Tribulation to take place. Well, everything God does has a purpose, so we can expect that the Tribulation will accomplish something important and specific.

- ✶ *To fulfill the prophecies about Israel.* Many prophecies about Israel have yet to be fulfilled, and some of them can only be fulfilled during the seven-year Tribulation.

- ✶ *To shake people from their false sense of security.* When everything is going great, people think they don't need God. Earthquakes, plagues, and other happenings during the Tribulation will shake people from that feeling. When they hear the good news of Jesus during these hard times, some of them will be more open to accept Him into their lives. God *wants* people to know Him and be with Him, even if He has to do something really drastic to get their attention.

✫ *To force people to choose Christ or Antichrist.* One major purpose of the Tribulation is to give the billions of individuals living at that time seven years of opportunity in which to make up their minds to receive or reject Christ.

What's Going to Happen?

Some people who have read the Left Behind series and the Left Behind: The Kids series have asked where we came up with such incredible stories. The answer is, straight from the Bible. You see, the book of Revelation contains details about the terrible Tribulation. We're going to take a closer look at events that will happen during this time.

The Seal Judgments of the Tribulation— Revelation 6

In Bible times, seals were used to close up a scroll. A spot of hot wax was dripped onto the closed scroll, then the sender's signet ring was pressed into the wax to form a mark. This seal assured that the message would not be opened before it reached the individual to whom it was sent. The scroll that's about to be opened here and begin the Tribulation can only be opened by Jesus Christ (the Lamb of God)—He's in charge! We call these first judgments of the Tribulation the "seal judgments," because they each happen as Jesus breaks a seal on the scroll.

The first four seal judgments are the four horsemen. List the color of each horse. Describe its rider and what each rider has the power to do.

1. 6:1-2—first horseman

color: _____

rider: _____

2. 6:3-4—second horseman

color: _____

rider: _____

3. 6:5-6—third horseman

color: _____

rider: _____

4. 6:7-8—fourth horseman

color: _____

rider: _____

At the opening of the first seal, the first horse and rider appear. On the first horse is Antichrist, who comes to conquer at the beginning of the Tribulation. We read that he is wearing a crown rather than wielding a sword or carrying arrows, which indicates he will conquer the world's governments by peaceful diplomacy rather than military might.

The second horse appears to indicate blood and death. The third horse indicates a severe famine, which often is the case following military conflicts (as mentioned in the two previous seal judgments). Money won't be worth much once this seal is opened. The fourth horse brings a severe judgment—a fourth of the earth will be killed.

After these four horsemen, a fifth seal is opened (Revelation 6:9-11). According to verse 9, who is under the altar?

the _____ of those who had been

_____ because_____

Another word to describe these souls is "martyrs." A "martyr" is someone who has been killed for what he or she believes in. The martyrs mentioned in verse 9 are crying out to God for revenge upon those unbelievers who killed them. They are told that the time for revenge has not come, but it will.

We've now come to the sixth seal. Read Revelation 6:12-16 and describe what happens.

a great _____

sun _____

moon _____

stars _____

sky _____

every mountain and island _____

All these terrible things will lead many people toward even further rebellion against God. The Bible tells us they will actually pray to the rocks and mountains to "fall on us and hide us from the face of him who sits on the throne and from the wrath of the Lamb!"

The 144,000 Witnesses—Revelation 7

The 144,000 people mentioned here are a special group called by God to share the good news of Jesus during the Tribulation.

What are these people called (verse 3)?

servants of _____

Who are they (verses 4-8)?

_____

_____

The Trumpet Judgments—Revelation 8 and 9

A trumpet was used in Bible times to signal a special announcement or the coming of a major event. These trumpet judgments certainly qualify as major events! Many of these judgments are similar to the ten plagues on Egypt.

Write down what happens at the sound of each trumpet.

first trumpet (8:7): _____

_____

second trumpet (8:8-9): _____

_____

third trumpet (8:10-11): _____

_____

fourth trumpet (8:12): _____

_____

We find the fifth and sixth trumpets in Revelation 9. On the fifth trumpet, another star falls from heaven, but this one, possibly Satan himself or a special angel, has the key to the bottomless pit, which he opens to let loose a great swarm of demonic locusts. These special creatures are permitted to torture—but not kill—people for five months. This will be a terrible time for unbelievers.

The sixth trumpet judgment releases four angels who are specially created for this moment in history. These angels command an angelic host of 200 million demons who go forth as horsemen to cause death upon a third of the people on earth. They, like the creatures in the previous judgment, come from the bottomless pit and are clearly not human. By this time in history, at least half of the earth's population will have died in only a few years.

But even after all these horrible things, the Bible tells us that people still won't turn to God! How did most people respond to these events (9:20)?

_____

_____

God's Two Supernatural Witnesses—
Revelation 11

God's love is so great that He will have the good news of Jesus proclaimed worldwide during the Tribulation. During the first half of the Tribulation, God uses the 144,000 Israelites from each of the 12 tribes who reach "a great multitude that no one could count" (Revelation 7:9), and He brings forth two special witnesses who have supernatural powers (Revelation 11). Let's look at who these two people are and what will happen to them.

How long will the ministry of the two witnesses last (verse 3)?

_____

What incredible powers will these two witnesses have (verse 6)?

_____

Describe what happens to the two witnesses after they finish their ministry (verses 7-8).

_____

_____

How do the evil people who hate the witnesses respond (verses 9-10)?

_____

_____

Something amazing then happens to the two witnesses. What is it (verses 11-12)?

_____

_____

The Antichrist—Revelation 13

In some places in the Bible, the word "beast" is used as a symbol for a government. However, the "beast" pictured in Revelation 13 is obviously a future world leader because he takes on the functions of a person. In fact, he is joined in this chapter by a "false prophet" who is also human.

We know that the Antichrist will be in power during all seven years of the Tribulation, and he will have almost total control of the people during the second half. We're about to see just what kind of ruler he will be.

In the Bible, "dragon" refers to the devil. What three things will the dragon (Satan) give the beast (verse 2)?

1. _____

2. _____

3. _____

What kind of following will the Antichrist have (verse 3)?

The _____ was astonished and _____

_____.

Who will the people of earth worship during this time (verse 4)?

1. _____

2. _____

What kind of power will the Antichrist have (verse 7)?

_____

_____

"Saints" in verse 7 refers to people who will come to believe in Jesus during the Tribulation (thanks to the 144,000 witnesses and the two supernatural witnesses).

What is God's challenge to the saints living during these days (verse 10)?

This calls for _____

and _____ on the

part of the saints.

The False Prophet—Revelation 13

Whenever a political leader tries to get rid of the true worship of God, he often begins by using the services of a false religious leader. The Antichrist will be no different. The Bible tells us another beast, this "false prophet," will come to power alongside the Antichrist. This leader will look "like a lamb" and speak "like a dragon" (verse 11).

Where will this leader get his power (verse 12)?

_____

What does he make the people of earth do (verse 12)?

_____

What other powers will the false prophet have (verse 13)?

_____

The Bible tells us this false prophet killed everyone who refused to worship the Antichrist (verse 15). He also forced the people of the earth to do something else—something you may have heard about. What is it (verse 16)?

To receive a _____ on his _____

or on his _____ .

What happens to people if they _don't_ have this mark (verse 17)?

_____

The number 6 is used in the Bible to mean "man." I've bet you've heard of the number for the beast. What is it (verse 18)?

_____

Lots and lots of people have tried to figure out what that number means. Truth is, we don't know. What we _do_ know is that this number is a clue for people during the Tribulation, to help them identify who the Antichrist is.

More details of the last half of the Tribulation are described in Revelation 16. Keep in mind that the bowl judgments we're going to talk about next will occur during the time Antichrist rules the world, with the false prophet as his religious leader.

The Bowl Judgments—Revelation 16

The bowl judgments, when compared to the seal and trumpet judgments, appear to be the most intense and severe. It appears that these bowls have been collecting God's wrath, so to speak, for a long time. Now they are filled to the brim and ready to be poured, which will prepare the way for Jesus' second coming. In the spaces below, describe what happens when each bowl is poured out.

first bowl (verse 2): _____

_____

second bowl (verse 3): _____

_____

third bowl (verse 4): _____

_____

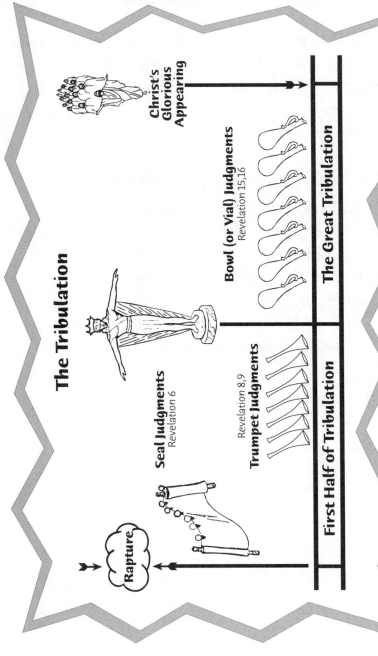

The Tribulation

Christ's Glorious Appearing

Bowl (or Vial) Judgments
Revelation 15,16

Seal Judgments
Revelation 6

Revelation 8,9
Trumpet Judgments

Rapture

First Half of Tribulation

The Great Tribulation

fourth bowl (verses 8-9): _____

_____

fifth bowl (verses 10-11): _____

_____

The sixth bowl is poured out "on the great river Euphrates" (verse 12) so that its flow of water dries up. This prepares the way for the kings of the East to come to the mountains of Israel for the battle of Armageddon (that's coming in Revelation 19). God is clearly baiting the Antichrist and drawing him into this location as a trap, which is set for further and final judgment at the second coming.

Good to Know

Armageddon will be the last great world war of history. The term **Armageddon** comes from the Hebrew language. **Har** is the word for "mountain." **Mageddon** is likely the ruins of an ancient city in northern Israel. The word came about because of *where* the battle will take place—on the plain of Esdraelon, around the hill of Megiddo, in northern Israel.

From the seventh bowl comes "flashes of lightning, rumblings, peals of thunder and a severe earthquake" (16:18). The next verse says this worldwide earthquake will cause Jerusalem to be split into three sections. This judgment is accompanied by 100-pound hailstones from heaven. And still, people will curse God instead of turning to Him.

Important Questions

The Tribulation is going to be the most horrible time the earth has ever known—more horrible than the ferocious battles in World War II, more horrible than the plagues that killed millions of people during the Dark Ages, more horrible than anything we've seen or can even imagine.

But here's the good news: God doesn't want people to have to go through this horrible time. He wants them to know Jesus. He wants them to ultimately spend eternity with Him. And so, even during these seven horrible years, people will still have a chance to turn to Jesus rather than the Antichrist. It's their last chance.

We're not in the Tribulation, but we should still ask ourselves: Will we turn to Jesus? Or will we reject Him? Where do you stand? As we close this chapter, it would be good for you to answer the following two questions.

⭐ Have you ever invited Christ to come into your life to forgive your sin and save your soul?

⭐ If so, when?

If you haven't or aren't sure, why not do so right now? A simple prayer of faith often goes something like this: "Dear Lord, I have sinned against You. I believe that Your Son, Jesus, died for my sin on the cross and rose on the third day from the grave. Please come into my life and forgive my sin. I give myself and my future to You."

If you have not prayed a simple yet sincere prayer like this, please do so and enter your name and today's date in the space below.

Name_____ Date_____

Then tell someone about your decision! It's the most important decision you'll ever make, so be sure to share it with others.

If you've already accepted Jesus before reading this book, I'm thrilled! It's great to see that you, as His child, want to know more about Him and His plan for the future.

Digging Deeper

Revelation is not the only place in the Bible that talks about the Tribulation. If you want to dig deeper, check out these verses!

Some Old Testament Tribulation References

The Time of Jacob's Trouble . . . . . Jeremiah 30:7

The Seventieth Week of Daniel . . Daniel 9:27

Jehovah's Strange Work . . . . Isaiah 28:21

The Day of Israel's Calamity. . . . . Deuteronomy 32:35;
Obadiah 12-14

The Tribulation . . . . Deuteronomy 4:30

The Day of Vengeance. . . . . Isaiah 34:8; 35:4; 61:2

The Time of Trouble . . . . Daniel 12:1;
Zephaniah 1:15

The Day of Wrath . . . . Zephaniah 1:15

New Testament Tribulation References

The Day of the Lord. . . . . 1 Thessalonians 5:2

The Wrath of God . . . . Revelation 14:10,19;
15:1,7; 16:1

The Great Day of the Wrath of the
Lamb of God . . . . Revelation 8:16-17

The Wrath to Come . . . . 1 Thessalonians 1:10

The Great Tribulation . . . . Matthew 24:21;
Revelation 2:22; 7:14

The Tribulation. . . . . Matthew 24:29

The Hour of Judgment . . . . Revelation 14:7

7

The Glorious Appearing

☆ ☆ ☆

Ryan approached Bruce after the meeting. "We're gonna be together now, right?" he said. "You and Vicki and Judd and everybody from now on."

Bruce put a hand on Ryan's shoulder. "I'd like to think we'll all see the glorious appearing of Jesus at the end of the Tribulation," he said, "but I can't promise. Many will die for their beliefs before Christ returns. It's already happening."

Death Strike

(Left Behind: The Kids #8)

☾ ☾ ☾ ☾ ☾

The most thrilling event in human history is coming soon. Jesus will return to earth and set up His kingdom that will last 1,000 years. We call this return the "glorious appearing." The more than 300 prophecies that speak of Christ's second coming guarantee it will take place.

Imagine what that moment will be like. What will Jesus look like? No one knows for sure, but we do know He will appear as God in human flesh, and He will be worshiped by both angels and men. To get a full picture of what this moment will be like, we need to put several prophecies together. Let's start with Jesus' own description of His glorious appearing.

There Will Be Signs

Jesus Himself said,

> Immediately after the distress of those days [the Tribulation] "the sun will be darkened, and the moon will not give its light; the stars will fall from the sky, and the heavenly bodies will be shaken." At that time the sign of the Son of Man will appear in the sky, and all the nations of the earth will mourn. They will see the Son of Man coming on the clouds of the sky, with power and great glory (Matthew 24:29-30).

Nature is going to tell the world Jesus is coming. People will see Him and pay attention.

Jesus Comes with His Saints to Judge

Enoch, the seventh from Adam, prophesied:

> See, the Lord is coming with thousands upon thousands of his holy ones to judge everyone, and to

convict all the ungodly of all the ungodly acts they have done in the ungodly way, and of all the harsh words ungodly sinners have spoken against him (Jude 14-15).

God revealed to Enoch that one day Jesus would come with thousands of holy ones to judge all humans. That judgment will begin with Antichrist, who will eventually be cast into the lake of fire.

Christ Will Stand on the Mount of Olives

Zechariah prophesied:

> The Lord will go out and fight against those nations, as he fights in the day of battle. On that day his feet will stand on the Mount of Olives, east of Jerusalem, and the Mount of Olives will be split in two from east to west (Zechariah 14:3-4).

After Jesus' crucifixion and resurrection, He rose into heaven *from* the Mount of Olives. Remember what the angels said to the disciples who were staring at the sky? "Men of Galilee," they said, "why do you stand here looking into the sky? This same Jesus, who has been taken away from you into heaven, will come back in the same way you have seen him go into heaven" (Acts 1:11).

Jesus will actually return to the same place, the Mount of Olives, and when His feet strike the Mount, that hill will split in two.

Christ Will Come as King of Kings

Of all the descriptions of the glorious appearing in the Bible, none is more vivid than what the apostle John viewed:

> I saw heaven standing open and there before me was a white horse, whose rider is called Faithful and True. With justice he judges and makes war. His eyes are like blazing fire, and on his head are many crowns…The armies of heaven were following him, riding on white horses and dressed in fine linen, white and clean…On his robe and on his thigh he has this name written: King of kings and Lord of lords (Revelation 19:11-16).

In verse 11, John sees a rider on a white horse. This is not the same rider of the white horse in Revelation 6:2, who will be the Antichrist. This rider, with eyes "like blazing fire," can be none other than Jesus. No longer is He lowly and humble, riding on a donkey (Zechariah 9:9), but He is the King of kings, riding in victory, power, and glory.

As a righteous warrior, Jesus will be unbeatable. He will consume all who are opposed to Him. And He will be a righteous judge, for His all-seeing eyes will reveal all truth about every person and nation.

Verse 12 tells us He will have many crowns on his head. This means He will come as one with supreme authority.

Verse 14 describes who will appear with Christ at His glorious appearing: "the armies of heaven." The armies of heaven include angels, Old Testament saints, Christians who have died, and people who become believers during the Tribulation. Note the clothing—fine linen, white and clean. No person would go to war in white because battles are so dirty and bloody, but our Commander-in-Chief has His army wear white because not one of us will lift a finger. Jesus will speak and the war will be won instantly!

The glorious appearing of Jesus will not only bring about the end of the Antichrist, his False Prophet, and the millions of people they deceived, but it will also bring about the beginning of the Millennial kingdom (we'll talk about that in the next chapter). This will conclude the seven-year Tribulation period and usher in the kingdom over which Christ will reign. At this time Jesus will judge the nations and decide who can enter the Millennial kingdom.

Revelation 19:16 tells us that "on his robe and on his thigh he has this name written: King of kings and Lord of lords." A warrior goes into battle with his sword on his thigh. Jesus' sword will be His spoken word. The word that called the world into being at creation will call every human leader and the world's armies into service to Him. Jesus, the living Lord, will be established in that day for what He is in reality—the King above all kings, the Lord above all lords. The prophet Zechariah said it best: "The LORD will be king over the whole earth. On that day there will be one LORD, and his name the only name" (Zechariah 14:9).

Amen!

8

The Millennial Kingdom

"You're right. But there's something else. Tsion wrote back and told me what he thought would happen after the Glorious Appearing. I mean, if Judd and I do get married, will we still be married after Jesus comes back? Could we have children? There's all kinds of questions, and the return of Christ is only a year away."

Shelly bit her lip. "Does make you think, doesn't it."

Vicki pulled out a copy of Tsion's e-mail she had printed and turned on her flashlight. "He's talking about people who will go into the millennium alive—

"What's the mill…milla…what you said?"

"A millennium is a thousand years. When Jesus comes back at the Glorious Appearing, he's going to reign a thousand years before the time of judgment."

"And the thousand years starts after the battle of Armageddon, right?"

"Exactly."

The Perils of Love

(Left Behind: The Kids #38)

There is an incredible time coming in the future. After the rapture, the Tribulation, and the glorious appearing, there is going to be 1,000 years *here on earth* when Jesus will be in charge. We call this the "Millennial kingdom" or the "Millennium."

Good to Know

The word Millennium is a Latin term that means "a thousand years."

Jesus will come to earth and set up His kingdom and rule for 1,000 years. During this time, He will be the focus of all creation, and He will rule visibly over the entire world in power and great glory. It will be a wonderful time in which righteousness and peace will rule the day.

This period of time is the beginning of the end of human history here on earth (only 1,000 more years to go!) and when it is done, we will then enter eternity.

Who Will *Not* Be There?

One person, who has made a mess of things here on earth, will *not* be around during the Millennial kingdom. Find Revelation 20 in your Bible and see who it is.

According to verses 1-3, who is bound and thrown into the Abyss during this 1,000-year reign of Jesus?

_____

Can you imagine earth without Satan?

A Wondrous Age

Since the fall of Adam and Eve in the Garden of Eden, humanity and creation have felt the effects of Satan and sin. Sin has tainted every human and all of creation.

However, during the 1,000-year Millennial kingdom, God will lift some of the effects of original sin, although there will still be death (for those who entered the Millennium in their natural bodies—believers who came to know Jesus during the Tribulation and survived to the end of the Tribulation). This coming kingdom will be a lot like the Garden of Eden. People and angels who rebelled against God will be gone. Satan will be tied up so he can't tempt man, and Christ, with the help of angels and believers, will enforce righteousness. Everyone will have their own home. The earth will bear incredible harvests. There won't be war or cheating.

Isaiah 65 tells us people will live as long as those who lived before the days of Noah. That means a believer who is born near the beginning of the Millennium could live to almost 1000 years of age! Isaiah 65:20 says a person will still be considered young at 100 years of age.

Because of these living conditions, the world population will grow, and it will be a happy time. In Zechariah 8:5 we read that the "city streets will be filled with boys and girls playing there."

A Time of Faith

Most of the population will be or become believers during this Millennial kingdom. Spiritual life will be unlike anything we've ever experienced. Living daily in the personal and physical presence of Jesus Christ will have an enormous impact on the lives of believers. The knowledge and worship of Christ will be worldwide. The Millennium will be an era of great spiritual awareness, sensitivity, and activity.

The government and politics of the millennial kingdom will focus on Jesus Christ. He will rule from Jerusalem (Isaiah 2:1-4), fulfilling God's promise to King David in 2 Samuel 7:12-16. God's covenant with David guaranteed David's dynasty, throne, and kingdom would continue forever. When Jesus Christ returns at the end of the Tribulation, He will reestablish David's throne (Jeremiah 23:5-8). God always keeps His promises!

A Rebellious Movement

Despite the ideal conditions, many will rebel at the end of the 1,000-year kingdom. Revelation 20 shows us that at the end of the 1,000 years, Satan will be loosed from the bottomless pit to go out "to deceive the nations"—that is, to tempt them to rebel against God. God allows this so that all the unsaved at that time will be forced to make a decision about Christ before eternity begins.

How many will rebel? Revelation 20:8 says there will be a multitude whose number is like "the sand on the seashore." This won't be all Satan's fault. People will choose to rebel, and Satan will simply bring to the surface the rebellion within people's hearts.

The End of Satan

After this rebellious movement, God is going to deal with Satan once and for all. Find Revelation 20 and see what happens.

Where is Satan thrown (verse 10)?

_____

What two other people will he be joining there (verse 10)?

1. _____

2. _____

(Remember, "the beast" is another name for the Antichrist.)

This is how it ends for evil: Satan, Antichrist, and the False Prophet will be thrown into the lake of fire, along with all those from history who rejected God's gift of salvation. The Bible clearly states that this punishment will last for all eternity!

Something to Look Forward To

Our world is filled with chaos, sadness, confusion, violence—but as believers, we have hope. We know that this world, the world we know, is not how it's going to be for all eternity. God has something wonderful planned for us. And part of that plan includes 1,000 years in a beautiful, almost-perfect world—before God brings in eternity.

9

The Very, Very, Very End

"We are engaged in a great worldwide battle with Satan himself for the souls of men and women. I do not say this lightly, for I do understand the power of the evil one. But I have placed my faith and trust in the God who sits high above the heavens, in the God who is above all other gods, and among whom there is none like him.

"Scripture is clear that you can test both prophet and prophecy. I make no claim of being a prophet, but I believe the prophecies. If they are not true and don't come to pass, then I am a liar and the Bible is bogus, and we are all utterly without hope."

Wildfire

(Left Behind: The Kids #27)

We've come to the end of the world. It's going to be a scary and sad time for people who haven't accepted Jesus. And it's going to be an incredibly wonderful and amazing time for those who love and follow Jesus. It starts with a judgment and ends with everything being made new.

The Great White Throne Judgment

Everyone knows that one day we will all stand before God and give an account of our lives. One reason many unbelievers say God doesn't exist is because they're afraid of facing Him at the judgment. However, the Bible is clear: "Man is destined to die once, and after that to face judgment" (Hebrews 9:27).

Judgment is taught in the Old and New Testaments. Jesus talked about it more than anyone else in the Bible (see John 5:22, Matthew 13:37-43). But the most vivid description of the ultimate judgment day is found in Revelation 20:11-15. This passage describes the Great White Throne Judgment, which occurs after the Millennium and just before eternity.

> Then I saw a great white throne and him who was seated on it. Earth and sky fled from his presence, and there was no place for them. And I saw the dead, great and small, standing before the throne, and books were opened. Another book was opened, which is the book of life. The dead were judged according to what they had done as recorded in the books (Revelation 20:11-12).

The Great White Throne Judgment comes at the end of the Millennial kingdom, after Satan has been let loose. At the time of this judgment, Satan, the Antichrist, and the False Prophet have already been thrown into the lake of fire. It is the last event before we enter into eternity.

On a flight from Salt Lake City to San Francisco I sat next to a salesman who said he had never read a Bible. I asked if he would try an experiment and he agreed. Turning to Revelation 20:11-15, I handed him my Bible with this brief instruction: "This is a prophecy about a future event." I waited as he read. His cheerful mood changed abruptly and soon he exclaimed, "If that's true, I'd better get right with God!"

That salesman put into words the main reason God has given so much information about the judgment that awaits all who reject God. God does not want people to face eternity in hell. He longs for people to become saved and live with Him forever in heaven.

Who Sits on the Great White Throne?

The Judge who sits on the Great White Throne is none other than the Lord Jesus Christ Himself. The Person who was rejected and scorned by men will ultimately sit in judgment on them. That is a sobering thought!

When Jesus walked the earth, He had an uncanny ability to look at a person and know him or her intimately. No one will be able to hide himself from the Savior's penetrating eyes on judgment day! As the Bible says, "There is nothing concealed that will not be disclosed, or hidden that will not be made known" (Matthew 10:26).

We know who the Judge is, but what about those to be judged? John reports in Revelation 20:12, "I saw the dead, great and small, standing before the throne." It's important that all who stand at the Great White Throne Judgment are "the dead"—or, dead in sin because they rejected Jesus. The phrase "great and small" means God will judge everyone fairly.

The Books Used at This Judgment

The Books of Man's Works. "And books were opened.... The dead were judged according to what they had done as recorded in the books" (Revelation 20:12). Evidently God owns a complete set of books that records every thought, motive, and action of a person's life, waiting to be recalled on judgment day. These are the books of man's works.

The Books of Life. Two books await every person about to be judged by God. The New Testament refers to the Book of Life eight different times, and although the Old Testament does not call it by that name, it does refer three times to a book in which names are written. The psalmist speaks of the righteous as having their names written in "the book of the living" (Psalm 69:28 KJV), so it is a book in which righteous people have their names written.

Revelation 13:8 tells us about the other Book of Life—"the book of life belonging to the Lamb." The Lamb is without doubt the Lord Jesus Christ, for only He is the "Lamb of God, who takes away the sin of the world" (John 1:29). People who have received eternal life have their names written in the Lamb's Book of Life.

During the Tribulation, those whose names are not written in the Lamb's book will worship the Antichrist and bear the mark of the Beast (Revelation 13:16). A person's eternal destiny, then, is based on whether or not his name is written in the Lamb's Book of Life!

The major difference between the two books is that the Book of Life seems to contain the names of *all living people*, whereas the Lamb's Book of Life includes only the names of those who call upon Jesus for salvation. A second difference is that the Book of Life is referred to as God the Father's book in Exodus 32:33. The Lamb's Book of Life is referred to as God the Son's book (Revelation 13:8). We may conclude, then, that this book contains the names of all those who have received the new life that the Son offers.

Anyone whose name is not found in the Lamb's Book of Life at the Great White Throne Judgment will be thrown into the lake of fire for all eternity. This will not be a pretty sight. But this does not have to be anyone's fate if they're willing to accept Jesus as Savior. For the Bible says, "Believe in the Lord Jesus, and you *will* be saved" (Acts 16:31, emphasis added).

Acknowledging Who Jesus Is

There is an awesome scene recorded in Philippians. The apostle Paul wrote this about Jesus:

> Therefore God exalted him to the highest place and gave him the name that is above every name, that at the name of Jesus every knee should bow, in heaven and on earth and under the earth, and every tongue confess that Jesus Christ is Lord, to the glory of God the Father. (Philippians 2:9-11).

Paul proclaims that there is a day coming when *every* knee should bow and *every* tongue confess that Jesus Christ is Lord. *All people,* not just believers, but even those who have rejected Christ will admit that Jesus Christ is Lord! This will probably happen at the close of the Great White Throne Judgment.

The Savior Is Waiting

If Jesus Christ had not come into this world to die for our sins, we would all be sent to hell. None of us is good enough for heaven. But because He loves us, Jesus paid the penalty and accepted total punishment for us. Our sins are completely forgiven and Christ's righteousness is given to us. Anyone foolish enough to pass up this free ticket to heaven is reserving a spot in hell.

In the archives of the U.S. Supreme Court is the record of a very strange incident that took place during the term of President Andrew Jackson. A man named George Wilson was sentenced to die by hanging for a crime he had committed. Somehow the story came before the president, who granted Wilson a pardon. To everyone's amazement, Wilson tore the pardon to shreds and threw it on the floor of his prison cell. The pardon had been refused. After long, legal arguments, the justices ruled as follows: "A pardon is a writing, the value of which is dependent upon the acceptance by the individual for whom it is intended." They decided George Wilson should be hanged until dead—because the pardon was not accepted.

This is a perfect picture of the sinner who hears the gospel of Jesus Christ and rejects God's pardon. If you are without the Savior today, it is because you choose to be. And we've seen, according to the Bible, where a life without Jesus will end up.

Everyone has a choice. We can admit we are sinners and invite Jesus Christ into our lives as Lord and Savior, or we can reject Him. Where we live in eternity will be determined by that choice. Those who have chosen to put their faith in Christ will rule and reign with Him during the 1,000-year kingdom and then go on into eternity with Him. Those who reject Him won't.

One of the clearest offers of salvation in all the Bible came from our Lord Jesus Christ Himself: "I tell you the truth, whoever hears my word and believes him who sent me has eternal life and will not be condemned; he has crossed over from death to life" (John 5:24).

Make that right choice today!

Welcome, Eternity!

After the Great White Throne Judgment, eternity will begin. Eternity will be so beautiful and perfect that it's hard to imagine! In case you've wondered what it will be like, God does tell us some exciting things about eternity in Revelation 21 and 22. Get your Bible and let's find out what's in store.

What two new places will be in eternity (21:1)?

1. _____

2. _____

What happened to the first versions of these two places (21:1)?

_____

What's different about the new earth (21:1)?

_____

After God does away with this planet as we know it, He will create a new heaven and a new earth. They will be better than anything this world has ever known, including the Garden of Eden.

He is also going to create a new Jerusalem (21:2). It's going to be a dazzling city, unlike any city we have ever seen. God Himself will be there with His Son and with the

Holy Spirit. This will make the new Jerusalem one grand and glorious place to worship.

In eternity, things will be very different from life on earth now. According to Revelation 21:4, what will no longer exist?

1. _____

2. _____

3. _____

4. _____

Amazing! Jesus proclaimed, "I am making everything new!" and He will. At the coming of the new heaven, the new earth, and the new Jerusalem, Jesus had this to say:

"It is done. I am the Alpha and the Omega,
the Beginning and the End."

Amen! Once we enter eternity, it is done. Jesus has completed all that He needs to do, and we'll just get to enjoy it with Him. You know how most fairy tales end with "And they lived happily ever after"? Well, this time, it's for real.

Jesus knows the plan for the world, for humankind, for you and me, from the beginning to the end, and He's going to see it through. You can trust Him for that. I don't know about you, but that makes me happy and excited about the future.

Final Words About Jesus' Return

People often ask me if I think Jesus is going to return soon.

I do.

Our changing world is incredible to watch. The terrorism and turmoil around the world show us how ripe conditions are for the end times.

People often ask me if I'm afraid of the future, knowing all I know about Bible prophecy.

I am not.

I know Jesus personally. He has saved me from my sins and has made some incredible plans for my eternity with Him.

I pray that upon completing this book, you will continue to study Bible prophecy to see what really is coming to pass. Then you won't have any reasons to fear, and you may begin to feel as I do—that Jesus could be coming soon.

May God bless you and may your heart be encouraged by all we have studied together in this book.